Façades are deceiving!

Foreword

Author Maita Floyd masterfully weaves the circumstances of the remarkable life of Marguerite, an attempted murder survivor. This true story will educate, delight, and sometimes even frighten you! With perseverance and grit, this former child of Nazi-occupied France must live with, and eventually overcome, a trauma so shocking that it was literally headline news. Along the way you will suffer with her and learn as this courageous woman grows from victim to survivor.

"Maita Floyd's third book vividly describes the nightmare behind the sensationalist headlines of attempted murder. The story is soon forgotten by the public but has lifelong repercussions for the victim.....this book captivates.....we share one courageous woman's life and her efforts to rebuild it after a few moments of terror nearly ended it."

Lurinda Schad,
Ahwatukee Weekly News, Phoenix, Az

"What a story it is! I could not put the book down. Her story should be an inspiration for every reader. Marguerite never allowed herself to remain a 'Victim of circumstance'....victim of another's senseless outrage.....Marguerite learned to survive."

John McComish,
Little Professor Bookstore, Phoenix, Az

DON'T SHOOT!

My life is valuable

by

Maita Floyd

Cover painting: Maita Floyd - self portrait
Cover design: Greg Stafford

Publisher's Cataloging in Publications
(prepared by Quality Books, Inc.)

Floyd, Maita, 1924 -
DON'T SHOOT! My life is valuable / Maita Floyd
p. cm.

1. Floyd, Maita, 1924 - 2. Victims of crime--United States--Biography. I. Title

HV6250.3.U5M35 1992 362.88
QBI192-1864

Library of Congress CIP 92-82711

Published by: Eskualdun Publishers, Ltd.
P.O. Box 50266
Phoenix, AZ 85076-0266

ISBN 0-9620599-2-7

To Willard

Maita Floyd

Since her retirement in the Ahwatukee area of Phoenix, Arizona, Maita Floyd has written and illustrated two books;

Caretakers, the Forgotten People,

Platitudes, You are not me!

An accomplished artist, the book covers are reproductions of her oil paintings.

Maita devotes much of her time to community service such as the AARP Widowed Persons Service as an outreach volunteer and grief support group facilitator.

In 1989 Maita represented Arizona as a Congressional Senior Citizen Intern in Washington D.C. Her name also appears in Who's Who of American Women.

Some of Maita's many affiliations include the Arizona Authors' Association, Arizona Book Publishing Association, National and Arizona Press Women, and the National Association of Women Business Owners.

Maita has been interviewed on numerous television and radio talk shows. She lectures nationwide and in Canada on the topic's of her books; Caregiving, grief, platitudes, and the emotional scars of attempted murder survivors.

ACKNOWLEDGMENTS

Many people have significantly contributed to this book. They are all very real, their names have been changed to protect their privacy. I owe many thanks to each and every person interviewed who was part of Marguerite's life;

Her New York neighbors, Kim and Joe, the Cramers and the Wagners, and her girlfriends, Mary and Gwen. Everyone of them touched her life in their own unique way.

A very special thanks to Gary W. Kriege, Director of Pastoral Services, Phoenix Interfaith Counseling, Phoenix, Arizona.

Excerpts reprint permission graciously extended by The Crown Publishers Group, publisher of Sweet Reprieve. The Charles Press, publisher of the 1991 winter issue of ICAL - Illness, Crisis and Loss. The Scottsdale Progress.

Grateful appreciation of the invaluable cooperation from my editors, Anna Marie Plagge and Greg Stafford.

CHAPTER 1

"You don't forget any of it
You just *heal* the memories
To forget would be amnesia."
Father Jenco (Hostage survivor)

In the sixties, Scottsdale was a little town bordering the east side of Phoenix, Arizona. It was known as "The West's most Western Town", a name the residents were proud of. It was also famous for its yearly "Parada del Sol", Arabian horse shows, dude ranches and Frank Lloyd Wright's Taliesin West. Scottsdale had a very diversified population with residences from mansions to modest ranch houses. The more expensive homes were found away from the center of town dotting the desert landscape and mountains. Scottsdale offered all the conveniences; schools, movie houses, theater, museums and shopping centers. Good restaurants were not hard to find especially in the exclusive hotels; the Biltmore,

Camelback Inn and Mountain Shadows. The most fashionable shops were located on Fifth Avenue. There was shop after shop of Native American jewelry, ladies apparel, and not to be forgotten, were the art galleries which, in those days, specialized in Western art. The best Western wear could be found at Saba's.

October brought winter visitors called "snow birds". They arrived by car, or planes from the northern, eastern and midwestern part of the country. Most of them were retirees fleeing cold temperatures and looking forward to the Phoenix area's balmy winters. All were happy to leave shovels and snow tires behind. Many of them resented the poetic and colorful label given to them by the Arizonians. The added winter population created a heavy concentration of shoppers and parking spaces were much sought after.

Each April the exodus began and the "snow birds" went home. By June, Scottsdale returned to a little sleepy town of 10,000. Left were the permanent residents, among them many artists. The city was theirs again. The main drag, Scottsdale Road, always avoided in winter, returned to its usual flow of traffic. No more bumper to bumper driving. Parking spaces abounded, even on Fifth Avenue.

Early morning, July 19, 1965. Children were still on summer vacation and mothers were already wishing that it was September and the start of another school year. Many residents were at their breakfast tables sipping coffee and reading the paper. In those days one could have the Scottsdale Daily Progress, an independent paper offering international, national and local news, delivered by a young boy on a bicycle, to one's driveway or doorstep. The cost of the paper was ten cents a copy or thirty cents a week. Homemakers scanned the ***Extra*** section in the Wednesday issues for the grocery specials.

Scottsdale Daily Progress

Monday ***July 19th*** ***1965***

Predicted temperature - 101 degrees, low humidity.

Normal for that time of year. Swamp coolers and air conditioners would soon be running at full speed.

The international and national headlines of the day;

Vietnam war...Vice-President Ford asks for, "Hard, bitter facts of the war."

Rusk at United Nations? Secretary of State Dean Rusk would welcome being appointed to fill the United Nations' Ambassador job vacated by the death of Adlai Stevenson.

But a local headline caught the attention of many readers on this day, July 19th, 1965, would send shock waves through the community.

Spouse shot; man charged

A Scottsdale man was arraigned in justice court today on a charge of assault with intent to commit murder in the shooting of his wife last Saturday.

Police said Thomas Anthony McGuire, 45, 7740 E. Heatherbrae, Apt 20, shot his wife Marguerite in the arm Saturday during a quarrel in their apartment. He was being held in lieu of $20,000 bond.

The shooting occurred about 2 p.m. Saturday. Police went to the scene after receiving an anonymous phone call and found McGuire sitting on a chair in the living room. His wife had fled to an adjoining apartment.

Mrs. McGuire told police that her husband stopped her when she tried to leave the apartment, they struggled and then he shot her after hitting her twice on the head with the pistol, a .25 caliber automatic.

Police found the pistol in the kitchen, a live shell in its chamber.

Police quoted McGuire as saying: "They said I was crazy."

Patrolman R. V. R........ reported McGuire said he received a letter from a lawyer stating that he was crazy, so he decided he might as well prove it.

Police said McGuire had alcohol on his breath. Mrs. McGuire was reported in satisfactory condition at Baptist Hospital.

How could it be? Here in Scottsdale?

In those days guns were not used in this peaceful town. They belonged to last century's lore of Tombstone, Doc Holiday, Wyatt Earp and Bat Masterson.

Was this a lovers quarrel?
What did she do to provoke him?
Was it infidelity?
Was he a violent man?

What happened to that woman? Who is she?

CHAPTER 2

"Whatever you can do
  or dream you can do, begin it.
For boldness has genius,
  power and magic in it."
Goethe

On a hot August day in the mid nineteen-twenties, in France, Felicie Branquet gave birth to a very healthy girl, her fifth child, Marguerite. At that time she could not perceive that Marguerite was going to be so unlike her other children. Being the fifth child influenced Marguerite's personality in many ways. Two more children were to be born after her and surrounded by older and younger siblings she felt stifled. To be different was important to Marguerite. She succeeded, but at times, to her detriment. She sometimes had to pay a high price with teasing from her siblings, frequent reprimands and rejection.

At a young age Marguerite showed signs of a very independent nature. She wanted to be her own person. She didn't fit into her maman's rigid mold and didn't live up to her expectations. Marguerite's inquisitive free-spirited nature was often repressed by the many restricting, "No, you may nots." She never heard enough of "Yes, you may." It seemed she always had one foot off the ground and Maman would say, "Marguerite, can't you walk? Must you run all the time? Why can't you behave like the others?" The answer was simple; she didn't want to, so she often escaped into a dream world because the real world didn't have much to offer.

Marguerite's parents, especially Maman, were always busy with their hotel, restaurant and large staff. Maman was a highly intelligent, shrewd, businesswoman and practically ran the hotel single-handed. Papa had time to pursue his many interests among them hunting. Marguerite was fascinated by his lengthy preparations for the hunting season. He never returned with an empty sack; pheasants, doves or rabbits always filled it.

Marguerite thought Papa was hers only. In her eyes he was so handsome, always impeccably dressed from his head to his toes, including his fashionable spats. Occasionally, she would find him in his favorite chair reading. She would climb onto his lap and be Papa's little princess. He would patiently answer her endless, "Pourquoi, Papa?" Those were rare stolen moments.

Papa enforced strict manners but corporal punishment was unheard of. A stern voice was enough.

At mealtime the children were not allowed to talk and had to eat everything on their plates. Marguerite found it difficult to repress all her questions but somehow managed, in order to please Papa.

The nurturing she longed for was left to a series of faceless maids, nannies or governesses. Until age ten, Marguerite was educated by a tutor. She didn't get the chance to meet or play with many children her own age except the neighbors, and her cousin Pierre. One year apart in age, they were inseparable. Their favorite game was playing marbles. Marguerite invented a game by putting a plank over the marbles. Balancing themselves on the plank was the object of that dangerous game. Many tumbles and scars were the result, but she didn't care! She was such a tomboy.

Due to his quiet nature, Pierre was unmercifully teased by Marguerite's siblings. They called him a sissy and told him he should be wearing girls' clothing. Marguerite enjoyed being with him because he never teased or told her that she was "clumsy" like her brothers and sisters did. She grew into a lonely child. A little princess, but emotionally an orphan.

Summers were the hotel's busiest seasons. The children's rooms were rented to hotel clients so they had to leave. It left Marguerite with a sense of not belonging and instability. Come July, Marguerite and her older sister, Therese, were sent to Tonton Joseph's until a villa could be built on some farmland her parents had bought, deep in the Pyrenees Mountains. It would be a suitable summer house for the children's use while Maman and Papa stayed in town managing the hotel. Each July, Papa drove Marguerite and Therese to Oregue, a little Basque village, where Tonton Joseph lived. Their car was probably the only one to be seen for weeks. The days were spent playing and running in the fields with her cousins. Tonton's woodmill provided seesaws for hours of fun.

Marguerite was never at loss to find new games. On one occasion they wanted to eat some ripe inviting apples from a neighbor's trees. There were some cows feeding in that field and a woman sat knitting, while tending them. One cousin said,

"Marguerite, say something to her in English she won't understand. It will distract her, we'll shoo the cows and she'll have to run after them."

They were all counting on her. Marguerite's limited English had been learned from the hotel guests who spent their winters away from England's inclement weather. What to say? Surprisingly at a loss for words, she screamed,

"Pig! Pig!"

It was the first English word that popped into her mind and it worked! The woman yelled back at her scaring the cows. As planned, they scattered across the field and she had to run after them. It gave Marguerite and her cousins enough time to get the apples. Forbidden fruit never tasted so good!

The following day, Marguerite and her cousins were walking along the main road. Monsieur Le Cure, the village priest, coming in their direction stopped them.

"Which one of you can speak English?" he asked.

None of them knew that the woman tending the cows had spent some time in England as a servant. Marguerite knew that the truth had to be told. It would be easier to admit it now rather than in the dark confessional booth.

With his most imposing voice he said,

"I will speak to your uncle and we will discuss an appropriate penance."

Tonton Joseph conveyed their joint decision,

"You cannot play with your cousins for two days!"

That was a harsh punishment for lively Marguerite. She would have preferred saying ten rosaries.

Everyday after lunch at Tonton Joseph's, a "sieste" was "de rigueur". Often not sleepy, Marguerite would escape into her dream world. She used the designs in the wallpaper to create her fantasies. A make-believe family was the theme, like the one she had always wanted to have. She imagined a papa going to work in the morning, and a maman who stayed home cooking and caring for the children. They would have endless conversations. She had quizzed one of the hotel employees about his home life. How envious she had been. Parents who would spend evenings together with their children. Real families! The hotel, the only home Marguerite knew, was elegant, had excellent food and many comforts - *yes* - but all that didn't bring happiness.

When she was ten, Marguerite and Therese, were sent to a boarding school thirty kilometers away, run by two spinster sisters. When Papa returned from driving them to the school for the first time he commented, "Marguerite didn't even cry!" Why should she? They were absentee parents and the school was just another place she was going to stay.

At the school they had to wear ugly black and white uniforms. When the students walked to church they could hear the other children calling them "the penguins". Marguerite often wanted to crawl into a hole rather than to hear those mocking words. During her stay at the school she received excellent grades. She was tutored by one of the teachers, Mademoiselle Durcudoy. A strong bond developed between them which would encompass six decades.

Three years elapsed. Maman selected a secondary boarding school in Pau, run by nuns. This one was a two-hour ride from the hotel. To Marguerite, it seemed very far away. Again, more rules and so many *don'ts.* Above all, she didn't like sleeping in a dormitory. Marguerite's mischievous nature often got her in trouble. Daily Mass was a bore, any student caught talking had to do verb conjugations during recess. Some of her favorite pastimes were saving cherry pits and throwing them at other students in study hall and sliding on the highly polished floors in her slippers when she was supposed to be in bed. Both of which were highly unacceptable behaviors for a young lady. Those innocent pranks made the stay bearable. How she missed Mademoiselle Durcudoy.

Marguerite's Godmother, a spinster, lived near Pau. It was a grey town so unlike the cheerful Basque villages with whitewashed houses and red tiled roofs. The townspeople were so cold compared to the obliging, spirited Basques. Maman decided that Easter Holidays would have to be spent with Tante Blanche, which left only the Christmas season to be spent at the hotel. What a bore! Again, daily Mass. Tante Blanche had a very nice apartment but nothing in it could be touched. How Marguerite longed for the vacations spent at Tonton Joseph's playing with her cousins. She was happy when the holidays were over and she could return to the convent.

By 1937, the family's country house was finished. It was a three story building with four bedrooms, one bath and two attic bedrooms for the servants. It had all the modern comforts except electricity, which didn't, as yet, reach that remote area. Maman hired Mademoiselle Durcudoy to be the children's teacher/governess and a cook/maid to care for all their needs. The special bond between Marguerite and Mademoiselle was rekindled. Marguerite, once again, felt loved and nurtured.

Those summers were idyllic and carefree. She had three months of fun playing on the monkey bars, trapeze, or the swing which Papa had installed. Endless games of pelota (Jai-Alai), were played with the neighboring farmers' children. Several times a week Mademoiselle would send Therese or Marguerite, pail in hand to a spring. According to Papa, the water was pure. She would despair when it was Marguerite's turn; it would take her forever.

Marguerite had built a dam to divert the water which, of course, needed regular maintenance and time was needed to look at insects and butterflies. For Marguerite, the world didn't exist beyond the perimeter of the villa, the huge garden and the stream. She had transported her wallpaper family to a quiet corner of the garden. Moss grew under the old oak trees, and there she built a Japanese garden like she had seen in one of Papa's fascinating books. Pieces of broken mirror would simulate water, twigs would make bridges. What a paradise! How she hated to hear Mademoiselle call. Back to reality!

On Sundays, Marguerite's parents could not spare the hotel chauffeur to take them to church. Mademoiselle and the children had to walk many kilometers on small paths to reach the little village church. How hard it was for Marguerite to sit still during those long incomprehensible sermons in Basque.

One of Mademoiselle's few rules was a daily walk. Often it would be along the dusty unpaved road which was bordered by blackberry hedges. Pails in hand they would gather berries. It was hard to tell how many more berries wound up in their stomachs than in the pails. Hands and tongues were always left black.

Mademoiselle had the patience of an angel. With Marguerite's impish nature she never knew what to expect next. Sliding down the banister was one of Marguerite's most cherished sports, although it was very *"unlady-like"*. In the living room stood a victrola. Marguerite's favorite record was, "Petit homme c'est l'heure de faire dodo", "Little Man it is Time to go to Sleep". Often Marguerite would not crank the handle fully so the song would come out all garbled. The result was uncontrollable giggling sessions with her siblings. The very conservative Basque farmers walking by with their flocks of sheep didn't approve of the crazy music coming out of the open windows of "le chateau", as they liked to call the villa.

Papa would regularly bring supplies. In the late 1930's, in that remote area, Papa's car was a novelty. If he had time, he would give the children rides in the rumble seat of his Fiat taking the corners sharply so they would fall on each other. What a treat!

To Marguerite, the only dark clouds during those summers were that Papa's visits, which she had so eagerly looked forward to, were much too short and she rarely saw Maman.

Summers don't last forever. Back to boarding school!

Chapter 3

"If we open a quarrel between the past and the present,
we shall find that we have lost the future."
Winston Churchill

1939 shook the Branquet family's peaceful life. War was declared against Germany by France and England. Rumbling thunder was heard coming from northern France. Marguerite's brother and her oldest sister's husband were mobilized. The year 1940 brought the defeat of France and drastic changes to their lives. First, the partial occupation of France by the Germans, followed by their requisitioning the hotel. Marguerite was devastated. She would no longer be able to walk into the hotel where she was born. How she had hated those "Boches" for the violation of her home. Even years later, she detested hearing German being spoken.

The family had to move to the villa. They were four difficult years for all of them. Marguerite started living with parents that she hardly knew. For practically a decade she had seen her parents only for brief times between stays at Tonton Joseph's, the villa and boarding schools. Now she faced daily, close contact with them. Her sister, Therese, left for the convent to be a nun. She was losing the sibling nearest to her age; the one who had been her protector and had sided with her when she got in trouble. Marguerite felt alone.

To a sixteen-year-old, Maman's religious beliefs of abnegation seemed so unreasonable. "You can't go swimming," Maman would tell Marguerite. "The war will end sooner." It was supposed to be a form of self-discipline and sacrifice, a sort of prayer for the end of the occupation. How could a teenager, an excellent swimmer, understand? All her friends could go swimming! Their strong personalities would often clash. None of Maman's other six children perplexed her like Marguerite. Surprisingly, Maman allowed her to take the year-long French Red Cross Nurse's training. It fit well with Marguerite's caring personality.

After graduation, Marguerite wanted to attend a nursing school, run by nuns, located in Paris. *No* was the answer; a severe disappointment. Again, she didn't understand Maman's decision. Marguerite was trying to make a future for herself, but Maman was making her own plans to find Marguerite a suitable husband.

This would be worse than death! Maman had made it clear that it would not be an easy task, after all, her daughter was a tomboy. Marguerite had often been told that she was not graceful but the most painful remark was when Maman had said with a despairing voice,

"I'll never be able to marry you!" Marguerite's self-esteem was crushed. Could she be that undesirable?

With a compelling sense of restlessness, Marguerite wanted to find a place in the sun, a life of her own, to escape from her confining middle-class environment. It would be better to leave than to marry a man picked by her mother.

> "I am incapable of a profound remark
> on the workings of 'Destiny'.
> It acts most generously toward people who
> nudge it off the road whenever they meet it."
> *West of the Night,* Beryl Markham

After the liberation, Marguerite heard that an American couple, the Lawrences, were looking for a French governess for their grandchildren, who lived north of New York City. Did she dare apply? Marguerite did and was hired on the spot. The Lawrences would sponsor her immigration. Her strong, adventurous, Basque ancestry gave her the will to override her mother's objections.

No one went to the railway station to see her off bound for Paris. Papa and Mamam had not even advised her younger sister, Sophie, away at boarding school, of her departure. They had not been able to say goodbye to each other. How cruel! After all these years Sophie still remembers the pain.

Recalling the past she fondly says,

"Oh, how I envied Marguerite. She went after what she wanted. She never gave up."

On November 25, 1946, Marguerite, barely twenty-two years old, boarded the S.S. America in LeHavre bound for New York. Conventions were thrown to the winds. She was off to find herself, to see new horizons and a world full of wonders! Before her departure, Papa, with what she thought was an air of envy and pride, had told her,

"You are doing the things I always wanted to do!"

The crossing was uneventful but arrival in New York harbor was spectacular! Passengers were summoned on deck. Lady Liberty was there, holding her torch, welcoming them as she had many others. From the distance, the Manhattan skyscrapers and the Empire State Building made an unusual background.

When Marguerite came from the suburbs to New York City on her day off she was fascinated by the many interesting and unusual sights. What a culture shock! The multitude of people walking up and down Fifth Avenue was quite different from where she was now living and her small summer resort hometown. Asking directions was quite interesting. Most of the policemen were Irish and they had a hard time understanding her high school English. Brogue versus a French accent! What did she ask? What did he answer? Still she always found her way.

Churches were a puzzle. In her hometown there was only one Church - Catholic. One Sunday she entered the first church she saw. Weird! No statues, a man preaching, people singing but, no Mass! It was quite a revelation that so many denominations existed.

Within a year, Marguerite realized that caring for children was not the job for her. She resigned and moved to New York City. Three days later she found a lady's companion job through an employment agency. At the agency a young woman, Bea, struck up a conversation with her. They had a lot in common as both had been in the United States only a short time. She invited Marguerite to have tea at her aunt and uncle's apartment located not far from the agency. Bea had not mentioned that they had a single son, Thomas. After tea he invited them both to the movies. For a lonely woman in a strange city the offer was welcomed.

After the movies Thomas showed quite an interest in seeing her again. He called several times to make a date, and finally in her loneliness, Marguerite accepted. She had met his parents, they seemed nice, and Thomas had a steady civil service job. She felt it would be nice to have someone to go out with. It didn't take long for Thomas to become serious and ask Marguerite to marry him. She was skeptical because their backgrounds were so different, but he was very persistent, and professed his love for her.

"During our lifetime, we are tossed *keys* to opportunities," says Beryl Markham in *West of the Night.*

We have the choice of catching them or ignoring them. Some keys look shiny like gold, the glare blinding. Often obstructed from view are many flaws. Circumstances heavily influence our decisions.

After many months of insistence, Marguerite accepted Thomas' proposal. A lonely, romantic girl, she convinced herself that she was in love.

Behind the *yes* were many reasons and driving forces. Her maman's voice ringing over the years, the haunting words, "I'll never be able to marry you!" were unforgettable. Years of teasing by her siblings, "You are clumsy, ugly, dumb", and her older brother's cruel remark, "Men don't like ugly legs," had taken their toll. Better say yes, another proposal might never happen! Her chances were slim. In the Basque region, "vieille fille", "old maid", was equivalent to,

"What's wrong with you?"

People would say,

"Pas encore mariee?", "Not married yet?"

If married, even a year after the marriage, "Pas d'enfants encore?", "No children yet?"

A very heavy legacy!

"Our childhood is a blackmailer"
unknown

CHAPTER 4

"Let there be spaces in your togetherness
Love one another, but make not a bond of love"
The Prophet, Kahlil Gibran

Marguerite and Thomas made plans for their marriage. She bought a beautiful full length bridal gown. In the spring of 1948 they were married in a New York City Catholic church. Mr. Lawrence gave the bride away. The ceremony was followed by a small reception in a club hall.

After WWII New York City apartments were scarce. After frantically searching for a place to live they settled in a very restricting furnished room. It was located near the Third Avenue elevated subway. Each time a train would pass by, everything would rattle. It would have to do until they found a better place. Luckily, several months later, their living conditions improved. Marguerite and Thomas found a cold water flat but it lacked many conveniences. The new location was very handy for Thomas as it was within walking distance to his job. Still their search for a better apartment continued.

Before the marriage Marguerite had quit her job as a lady's companion, she needed to find a less consuming work. One day, walking along Fifth Avenue she saw a "Help wanted" sign in a shoe store window. She inquired, found that a file clerk was needed, and was hired. No one would know if in her mind she would use French instead of English, same alphabet. The salary was $35 a week. Within a short time her supervisor, pleased with her work, gave her a raise.

In the fall of 1948, Marguerite became pregnant. Looking forward having her first baby, she quit her job to be a mother and housewife. That was her dream. It was shattered however, when she suffered a miscarriage. She was devastated. The usual platitudes were given, "You are young", "You can have more children."

None of these helped Marguerite to deal with her grief. Thomas didn't seem overly concerned. Marguerite mourned silently.

As soon as Marguerite was well she searched for another position. It didn't take long, even with her heavy French accent. She landed another job as a file clerk in an office located near Rockefeller Plaza. In the winter she often spent her lunch time watching the ice skaters or browsing through Sachs Fifth Avenue department store.

A year later Marguerite was pregnant again. However, her happiness and hopes were short-lived as this one, too, was terminated by a miscarriage. Her sadness was overwhelming. Though she had a close friend, Mary, that she shared many things with, confiding in another something this personal, was contrary to her upbringing. Marguerite repressed her grief. She had no one to give her comfort or listen to her pain.

Thomas was not solicitous. It would have been futile for Marguerite to express her emotions. Far from being a bad person, he would not have understood. Their communications were shallow. Thomas had a hard time dealing with anyone's feelings except his own, and those he generally kept to himself. Until he got married at the age of twenty-seven, he had lived with his parents. His mother had pampered and doted on him. She was the center of his world. Thomas was the youngest of four children, preceded by three girls. In that environment he never had the opportunity to learn to think of others. Mary remembered him as *selfish.*

At long last Thomas and Marguerite found a decent apartment in a quiet, mostly German, section of Brooklyn. Hard working Thomas set out to paint and wallpaper and it turned out to be a very cheery place. Soon after the move Marguerite realized that the apartment was much too close to his mother. Thomas insisted that most Sundays be spent visiting his parents. During the visits Thomas' dad never talked much. He was a quiet and very passive man. Marguerite and his mother got along well enough. She even told Marguerite that she was lucky to have such a nice daughter-in-law. But Marguerite soon got tired of those weekly visits. There were many other interesting to do; the movies, visiting museums and during the summer going to the beach.

Marguerite quit her job in the city and searched for one in her neighborhood. Within a couple days she landed a clerk position within walking distance of the apartment. Now she was a clerk - not just a file clerk. Advancement!

Many planes would fly over the office on their way to land at La Guardia Airport. Marguerite dreamed of being on one of them on her way to France. She revealed to Thomas her longing to visit her family in Europe. He was agreeable to the idea, but even though Marguerite was very thrifty, their combined salaries didn't leave enough money to save for the trip. She sometimes felt frustrated and disappointed at Thomas' lack of drive and ambition. Even when the opportunity was offered to take free classes to upgrade his job, Thomas didn't take advantage of it.

Their marriage was rather sedate. In her heart Marguerite still longed for children. In 1951, again she was given a ray of hope. She was pregnant. The doctor suggested bed rest so she quit her job but it was to no avail. A third miscarriage! Sadly, Marguerite would ask herself, "Why, why can't I carry those little babies to term?" Thomas didn't say much about the miscarriages. Could it be that children would have taken too much of Marguerite's time and affection? Without knowing it Marguerite was taking Thomas' mother's place. He was very comfortable in that kind of relationship.

Thomas was a nice fellow, hard working and kind but they were very ill matched. In spite of their differences, arguments were kept to a minimum. Keeping the status quo was good enough for him and Marguerite simply kept her thoughts to herself. The marriage was a mistake that Marguerite had a hard time admitting to herself and she certainly could not admit it to her family. They had always seen her as a failure. She could imagine their comments and their scorn, "She can't even make a success of her marriage!" She was determined to make the marriage work despite all the odds.

When she felt better Marguerite began searching for another job. She remembered seeing that huge TWA calendar in the office where she had worked before. Often her eyes had been drawn to those beautiful, enticing, three red letters. She would close her eyes and see herself flying toward France in one of those white airplanes. How she dreamed! Was is not true that one of airline employees' benefits was reduced air fare? Slowly an idea germinated. Why not try?

February 1952

Marguerite went to TWA's employment office located at La Guardia airport. Upon entering, she was greeted by a charming woman, Ms. Lyons,

"What kind of work are you looking for?"

"Clerical." replied Marguerite

"Can you type?"

Boldly Marguerite answered, "Some."

A text was given to her to type. When Marguerite handed the finished paper to Ms. Lyons she commented,

"Good work, but a little slow. Tomorrow report to Ms. Halmon, the TWA Sales Manager. Her office is located in the New York City airlines terminal. The position is typist-clerk and pays $175 a month."

What a "tour de force"! Boldness had landed the job. Marguerite was overjoyed and never divulged the fact that she had never taken a typing lesson. She compensated by using her visual abilities, memorizing a sentence then typing it while looking at the keys. Ms. Halmon, a retired Marine sergeant, was a tough boss but fair. It was a very pleasant office to work in.

Marguerite had always found apartment living too confining. She dreamed of owning a little house in the suburbs with a backyard, trees and flowers. A place of her own! She discussed it with Thomas and he was not opposed to the idea, neither was he very enthusiastic. Where could they find the money?

Providence came from Marguerite's parents who, at that time, gave $5,000 as a gift to each of their children. She was ecstatic! A down payment for a house! They bought a car and spent most weekends looking for a house on Long Island. A pre-WWII house was found that reminded Marguerite of France with its bay windows and wood paneling. It was rather quaint. Some of her dreams were becoming reality. She was relatively happy. It would be a wonderful place to bring up children. Deep down Marguerite was relieved that they were moving away from *Mom.* After the move she and Thomas didn't visit his parents as regularly. They had a house to decorate and furnish! It would take a lot of their time.

What wonderful neighbors they had! On one side lived an older couple with adult children and on the other side lived Joe and Kim who had several young children. Marguerite knew Joe from work. He was the manager of a New York City TWA office.

This was living! The problems in Marguerite's marriage were overshadowed by the happiness of moving into their newly acquired house. It gave her a sense of security and stability which was very important to her after being shifted from the hotel to her uncle's country house and boarding schools.

Marguerite's new life consisted of commuting to work and being a housewife. A year later she was pregnant. Marguerite's hopes soared again. Five months later she gave birth to twin girls who lived a couple of hours. Marguerite was heartbroken, her sorrow had no bounds.

Her neighbor, Kim, was kind and understanding. Marguerite was able to confide in her. It was useless talking to Thomas! She took all those miscarriages as personal failure.

Kim recalls,

"They had an argument. Marguerite wanted to have the twins baptized. Thomas didn't think it was necessary. He was ready, like he had told me, to *flush* them. He had no concept or notion of her hurt, or sadness. He was too self-centered and egocentric. She finally got her way and the twins were baptized. Marguerite would often come to the house alone. She seemed a happy enough person, very outgoing, easy to meet. She had a better time when he was not around."

After the loss of the twins, Ms. Halmon placed Marguerite on a three-month leave-of-absence. When she felt well enough she could search for an office job within the TWA metropolitan area. During her leave, Joe offered Marguerite a job in his office,

"I knew of her problems but she was ambitious and kept going. I promoted her knowing she would do well. I could not see any possibility of Thomas keeping up with her. I had the impression that he had married up, above himself. I thought he was happy, devoted, realizing that he had someone that he really should not have aspired to. It probably made him a little uncomfortable.

Thomas was a nice enough fellow, always ready to give you a hand if you needed it but he was opinionated, superficial and not very smart. I stayed away from him as much as possible. She had friends, I don't how many he had."

With a sad heart Marguerite gave up trying to have children. There was an alternative, adoption. She talked it over with Thomas and he was agreeable. Marguerite knew that the possibilities in the United States were very slim. Rarely were children available to a family with a working wife. Marguerite found a solution. A child could be adopted in France and brought, as theirs, to the United States. She had done her homework and had obtained the information from the United States Immigration Office. Happily, Marguerite contacted the old family doctor, Docteur Giraud in France. He soon answered with wonderful news. He had found a little two-year old boy ready for adoption.

Docteur Giraud commented,

"He even looks like you, same complexion."

Overjoyed, Marguerite could not contain her excitement. Eagerly anticipating his possible arrival, she started making plans. But in her euphoric state of mind, she had forgotten her mother-in-law's awesome influence on her son.

Thomas and his mom had been talking. *Her decision* was handed down through Thomas who said,

"If you can't carry your own, we won't have children."

Marguerite was floored, why should she interfere? Her hopes were torn to shreds by *that woman*. Marguerite knew his mother's dominant nature but, to that point! She was very angry, disgusted and revolted. Thomas had no back bone. Was it also because deep down he wanted a childless marriage? A child would interfere in their lives. The unseen cracks in the marriage were getting wider.

July 1957

Thomas had a job related accident, hurting his back. It was followed by a two-week stay in the hospital. Workmen's compensation became his only source of income. In order to make house payments, Marguerite came upon the idea of sharing the house with another couple. She felt that it would be a stop gap until a smaller and more affordable house could be bought. Marguerite's dream house had been purchased with enough room for an extended family, now those hopes were gone. A year later they sold the house for a profit and moved into a less expensive house for just the two of them.

Joe later said,

"They moved away. Marguerite had a good head for business. The buying and selling of fix-up, so-to-speak, houses, I am sure was her idea."

Eventually, Thomas was retired with a disability pension. He was not an invalid and could function well except that he could not do any sort of lifting. With the retirement came restrictions. Should he choose to work, his yearly additional income would be limited.

Marguerite had become the primary wage earner. Her job was her salvation, her security blanket, her co-workers an extended family. Work was a relief and distraction from her personal problems. It had always sustained her emotionally and given her a sense of purpose. She was now eager to advance. A ticket agent position would bring a good pay raise and a nice promotion. She heard that TWA, at Idlewild Airport, happened to be looking for a French speaking person to train as an agent. Joe had been promoted and her new supervisor, Robert Schmidt, discouraged her from applying saying,

"Passengers are not going to like your accent, it is too pronounced. You will have to lift luggage. And after all, you've had miscarriages, it won't be good for you."

He went on with his discouraging comments,

"It's a man's job. They already have one woman and are unlikely to hire another."

"Let me be the judge of that," retorted Marguerite. "Please, give me the time off and the opportunity to be interviewed."

Two days later she had an appointment with the airport manager. After presenting her credentials, she was immediately hired. Marguerite had obtained the job she had set her sights on. After a week's training she was facing her first line of passengers. Scary! It didn't take long for her to feel comfortable with her new responsibilities and to fit right in as *one of the boys.* Commuting to the airport was not always easy, especially when the roads were icy.

December 1958

Thomas' physician, Doctor Levine, suggested a laminectomy. It would eliminate most of his back problems. The operation was successful, but Thomas would have to be in a body cast for a month. This added to Marguerite's many other duties and work load. Before leaving for work she needed to bathe and dress him. The housework, shopping, and winter snow shoveling were now all hers.

Fall 1959

Thomas and Marguerite's neighbor, Sam, asked them if they would be willing to sell their house. His parents had just retired and he wanted them to move next to him. As the offer would bring another profit, it was readily accepted. They bought a fairly new, lovely, Cape Cod house.

In early 1960, Marguerite's older sister, Germaine, wrote her asking if she would be willing to sponsor her young son, Danny, to come to the United States? She hoped that he would have a better chance for a career in

New York. When he was a child, Marguerite had been his favorite aunt. Marguerite thought that was a fine idea and Thomas agreed with the decision. Late that year, Danny became part of their household.

It was not long after his arrival that problems arose. Thomas resented their closeness. He was jealous. Marguerite was delighted to have a teenager around her, someone with whom she could talk in her native tongue. Thomas would get angry when he heard Marguerite and Danny speaking French. He felt left out and it added to his jealousy. At times, Thomas made Danny's life unbearable. Marguerite was caught in the middle.

In 1961, Thomas' doctor suggested that moving to a warmer climate would be very beneficial for his back. Thomas agreed with the idea and Marguerite welcomed the doctor's suggestion. Furthermore, and best of all, thousands of miles would separate them from *Mother.*

Marguerite's job made the possibility of moving easier as she could apply for a transfer. But, where to go? She spread out TWA's continental routes map on a table. There weren't many choices. Only three cities on the map offered a warm, dry climate; Las Vegas, Phoenix and Tucson. Las Vegas was immediately eliminated, Marguerite didn't like that city. Tucson was a small station and probably would not hire a woman. Phoenix it would be!

In the sixties, women airport ticket agents were still a rarity. What sort of chance would she have with a transfer request? Phoenix seemed so far away, so remote from New York. To Marguerite, it was practically a foreign country. She was well traveled but had never been to the Southwest. Again, she relied on her usual boldness. Why not try?

On her days off, Marguerite flew to Phoenix. Upon her arrival, she sought the manager's office. She explained to the receptionist the purpose of her visit, and waited as she went into his office. Through the open door Marguerite heard a booming voice,

"Why in the h..l didn't she make an appointment?"

"Send her in."

Marguerite ventured into his office. Without ceremony she was told,

"Sit down",

"Why didn't you fill out the transfer forms?"

"Because I am a woman," replied Marguerite.

No sooner had those words passed her lips than he slapped his desk, roaring,

"I can see that!"

Marguerite knew right away that they would get along. Making eye contact she boldly replied,

"The application form has a space for sex, and I thought that if you saw 'F' in that spot it would probably mean that the form will end up in 'File 13'."

He liked her honesty and straightforwardness.

"I'll send my decision to your supervisor."

By his smile and strong handshake Marguerite knew

that the transfer was in her pocket. Upon her return to work at Idlewild Airport, the approved transfer was waiting for her.

Their plans were made, Marguerite would fly ahead and Thomas would remain in New York with Danny until the house was sold, then they would drive across the country to Phoenix. Later, Danny admitted that it had been a very difficult journey, with Thomas pouting most of the time.

April 1962

Marguerite left New York for her new life in Phoenix. She had good feelings about it. She had liked the open spaces seen on her first visit. The flight was to be unforgettable. Her pass privilege allowed her to fly first class if room was available. That day she was in luck! The aircraft made its scheduled stop in Chicago and all passengers disembarked except one man in the first class section and several in coach. A ticket agent came to check the meal status with the hostess.

All of a sudden, Marguerite heard her name called.

"Marguerite, what in the world are you doing here?"

It was Rick, a fellow employee who had transferred to Chicago from Idlewild. She explained the purpose of her trip. They talked about *remember when* and caught up on co-workers' activities, all that little non-hurtful airport *gossip.* As soon as Rick left, the other passenger stood up. Extending his hand, he introduced himself,

"I'm the Governor of Arizona. I overheard your conversation. May I be the first person to welcome you to our state."

A rare, unusual, and exceptional greeting.

At the arrival gate in Phoenix, the governor deplaned first followed by a smiling Marguerite. A band was playing on the tarmac. What a reception! It was to celebrate the arrival of the first aircraft at the newly built Terminal Number 2. Life was getting interesting.

Marguerite bought a second-hand car and found an apartment. Her search for a house would start immediately. In no time at all, she had adjusted to her new life and surroundings. She enjoyed the exceptional weather and mostly relaxing at poolside. No more commuting on the crowded Long Island parkways. This was life!

Another agent, Burt, had transferred the same month from the East and had also rented an apartment in the same building. As soon as he found a house, his wife and child would join him. Both low in seniority, Marguerite and Burt worked the three to midnight shift so they decided to go house hunting together. They made quite a game of it.

Their acting was played to such perfection that the salespersons all assumed they were a married couple. Dead-pan, Burt would say,

"Honey, I don't like this kitchen."

Marguerite would reply,

"Well, Dear, buy another house if you wish!"

Their bantering would drive the salespeople crazy and often left them dumfounded.

Burt had, at times, a wonderful and unusual sense of humor. One morning Marguerite was happily cooking her breakfast, kitchen window opened to let the spring air come in. All of a sudden a bugle sounded just outside her window. Eggs and bacon flew up in the air and landed in a scrambled mess on the floor. Burt had done a good job of scaring her but one could never stay angry with him for long. Those were carefree days that she had not known for a *very* long time. Marguerite enjoyed them to the fullest.

Eventually, Marguerite found a townhouse with a common pool that she liked very much, but waited until Thomas arrived to make a final decision. He liked it. As soon as the papers were signed they moved into their new Scottsdale home. Thomas refused to have Danny stay with them. He was adamant about it, and there was no swaying him. Thomas even went as far as forbidding Marguerite to see him. She was not about to comply.

Danny was in a strange city alone. Marguerite helped him find an apartment and drove him around town job hunting. His English was limited but he was resourceful like his aunt. He landed a job as a busboy. Marguerite kept in touch with Danny, although receiving his phone calls caused heated arguments with Thomas. Marguerite felt that Thomas was being unreasonable and she was often upset. She did her best to ignore her marital problems by keeping busy with work, swimming, and making new friends. As usual, Marguerite kept her life private, and didn't discuss her difficulties with her co-workers.

Her work at Sky Harbor Airport was a pleasure. The frenzied pace of Idlewild became a thing of the past. One day, a tall passenger approached the counter dressed in Western clothing from the ten-gallon hat on his head to the fine leather cowboy boots on his feet. He greeted her with a resounding,

"Howdy, Ma'am!"

Marguerite was floored!

What kind of a accent was that?

She was amazed by the easy going attitude of most passengers. Rarely did she see people running in the terminal. What a relief from working back East.

At the airport, Marguerite met Mark, a very engaging man, who owned one of the airport gift shops. During one of their conversations they discovered that his wife, Irene, and Thomas had the same ancestry. A date was made for the following Sunday for Marguerite and Thomas to visit the Cramers at their house.

Irene recalls,

"Thomas came by himself, Marguerite would join us after work. It was a pleasant evening. I was surprised at the difference between the two of them, not only in appearance but in intelligence. I thought that her husband would have been more sophisticated. My first impression was that she was worldly. I was very much interested in her background, the Basque people and the war years.

When our friendship flourished, I asked her if she had any children. Her miscarriages had made a big impression on me. She had faced a lot of adversities. I didn't pity her, but felt badly for her. I was delighted to know that she had a poodle named Youki that she doted on. It was her baby and I understood. At that time I was pregnant and felt great empathy for her. She seemed such an efficient business woman. I admired the way she handled Thomas. I never said much, but remember one day asking her why she had married him. She didn't answer."

Mark added,

"When I first met them it seemed like a mismatch. Marguerite was trying to bring him along, perhaps interest him in working for me at my other store in town. It was summertime and business was very slow, I could not afford to even employ a cat! Thomas started visiting my other shop regularly. I enjoyed it as there were few customers. I had no one else to talk to. One day a delivery truck arrived, and he helped me unload. I told him, 'I can't pay you'. He indignantly replied, 'Who asked for money? You are doing me a favor. It gives me something to do'. I didn't like people working for me and not getting paid."

Often, at lunchtime, Mark would go to the nearby coffee shop. He told Thomas that the owner's wife, Beth, was French and that Marguerite would probably enjoy meeting her. Later, Thomas made a habit of going to the coffee shop where he had met Beth. She found him nice enough.

"Why haven't you told me that your wife is French?" she one day asked him. She could not understand why Thomas didn't want her to meet Marguerite. Beth asked Mark, that if he ran into Marguerite at the airport, to tell her that a Frenchwoman wanted to meet her.

"At long last," recalls Beth,

"Marguerite came alone to the coffee shop and introduced herself. We were both delighted to meet someone with whom we could speak in our mother tongue."

"I found it strange," continued Beth, "that Thomas would not let Mark pay him. His wife worked and he didn't do a thing to earn money. Later I realized that Marguerite was *not happy.* I guess that she didn't want anybody to know that the marriage was not working."

In October, Mark offered Thomas a job. By then, he knew his way around the shop and was very familiar with the stock and was good at packing. Business had picked up so Mark decided to pay him.

"I told you no!" said Thomas.

"I don't want to get paid, no argument."

Mark put the check away and started counting Thomas' hours.

Early in December, Mark called Marguerite,

"What do you think Thomas would like for Christmas?" he asked.

She mentioned a slide projector that he wanted. Mark bought the best money could buy and gave it to him. Thomas was very appreciative and pleased with the gift. Mark recalls that, in December, things started to fall apart between Marguerite and Thomas.

During the holidays, it was customary for Phoenix airline employees to have a joint 'interline' party. Spouses were always invited and most of them attended. In December of 1964, Marguerite had asked Thomas if he wanted to go to the Christmas party. He had not responded. The day of the party, Marguerite asked again. She was not surprised by his answer,

"No."

Over the years Thomas had not wanted to attend parties involving her co-workers.

"I'll go alone." she airily said.

Angrily, Thomas retorted,

"We might as well separate!"

Marguerite's comeback was fast,

"Fine!"

Furiously, Thomas snapped back,

"I have to call Mom, you are going to kill her."

Not again, thought Marguerite, *Mom's* iron control is still in effect long distance.

Immediately, Thomas was on the phone calling his mom! Marguerite heard his whining voice,

"Mom, she is leaving me!"

But this was a joint decision! One very much welcomed by Marguerite. She left alone for the party. After that evening, their relationship became very tense.

A week later, upon returning home from shopping, Marguerite was greeted at the arcadia door by Thomas brandishing a bottle.

"I have taken poison. I'm going to kill myself."

Very upset, Marguerite tried to take him to the hospital but was unable to reason with him. In desperation, she called their parish priest, Father Smith, who convinced Thomas to go to the hospital with him.

Earlier that same day, Thomas had called Beth, who hardly recognized his low voice.

"Is that you, Thomas?"

"What's going on?" asked Beth.

"Things are not going well," replied Thomas,

"I'm looking for Marguerite, I'm sick."

"Can I do anything for you?" asked Beth.

"No" answered Thomas,

"Do you know where Marguerite is?"

"No, I haven't seen her for a couple of days"

Beth quickly answered.

Three days later, without being officially discharged, Thomas walked out of the hospital. The little boy who had been pampered by his family was again seeking attention. He had not swallowed enough Carbon Tetrachloride to hurt himself badly.

"The day Thomas left the hospital, Marguerite came to our house without her poodle," recalled Irene. "She was frightened by Thomas' behavior and asked Mark to pick up the small German sword which was hanging on the wall of their living room. Thomas had brought it back after WWII from Europe. She was afraid Thomas might use it to harm himself."

When Mark arrived at the house, the door was ajar. He pushed it open and heard Thomas talking to his mother on the phone.

Mark remembers,

"He was acting very immature, telling his mother that he was going to do something to himself. I thought, '*You jerk!'* That poor little old woman, what is she going to do for you? You've already tried it. I walked in and stayed for a while thinking, 'This is crazy, why am I keeping this man company?' Disgusted, I left."

Marguerite had enough of Thomas' dramatic behavior. She insisted that he move out. Any attempt at leading a normal life, for Marguerite, became a thing of the past.

After the divorce papers were served to Thomas at his apartment, he started harassing her. He constantly called Marguerite asking her,

"Why can't I come back?"

"Why do we have to get divorced?"

He sounded like a little boy who had lost his mother. Even though the phone calls were not threatening, Marguerite was fearful.

During that time, Thomas was also regularly calling the Wagners and the Cramers. He thought Marguerite was hiding at their houses. He always wanted to know where she was, imagining that she was having an affair.

Irene recalls,

"After that airline party he was obsessed with the idea that Marguerite had a boyfriend at work. He was very insecure. She was weary of his behavior and had him served with restraining orders. Marguerite hoped that those official papers might influence Thomas to behave and leave her alone. She knew that the police could not possibly offer twenty-four hour surveillance. She only wanted some semblance of peace in her life. After all, Thomas had agreed to the separation, but he was stunned and could not believe that Marguerite would actually follow through with the divorce."

Chapter 5

"It is not a dream, it's a memory,
but substantial enough
that it can't be willed away."
Hard Fall, Ridley Pearson

May 1965

Thomas left Phoenix bound for New York. He was going to live with his mother. Marguerite let out a sigh of relief, she had a taste of freedom. Now she would be able to peacefully go to work and start a life alone. Coming home after her twilight shift, she looked forward her poodle's excited welcome and the silence. Marguerite had led so many years of quiet discontent. Now she thought she could become her own person. It was so pleasant taking her daily leisurely swim in the pool and resting without having to think of what Thomas was going to do next!

July 17th

A day like any other day of her new life, Marguerite got up late. After lunch it would be time to get ready for work. Marguerite never had a wardrobe decision, she would wear her airline uniform. Around 2:00p.m., car keys in hand, Marguerite opened the arcadia door leading to the pocket-size garden where she had planted some shrubs and her favorite flower, rose bushes. As she stepped out, like a cheetah stalking its prey, Thomas sprang out of the bushes.

Startled, and completely taken by surprise, she managed to ask,

"What in the world are you doing here? I thought you were in New York with your mother!"

"Get in," he barked, pushing her into the living room.

He pulled a gun out of a paper bag and brandished it in front of her face.

A GUN ?

Marguerite had never seen a handgun before.

She could not believe it!

"He can't be serious," she thought.

During their years of marriage, Thomas had never shown any signs of violence.

"Please, put that thing away!" exclaimed Marguerite. It was beyond her comprehension that he intended to use it. For what reason?

Thomas waved a paper in front of her.

"You think I'm crazy?" he shouted.

"What are you talking about?"

"These divorce papers!" he shouted wildly.

Aghast, Marguerite reached for the nearby phone,

"I have to call work, let them know I won't be in."

In a rage, Thomas screamed,

"That's right! You'll never work again!

If I can't have you nobody else can!"

In a trance, Marguerite sat down to call her supervisor. While dialing she was praying, desperately trying to think of something to say that would arouse his suspicion. She had never called in to miss work at the last minute. When he answered, lamely she could only say,

"I won't be in today," offering no excuse.

"OK," was the laconic answer, and sadly, she heard the click. Her attempt for help had gone unnoticed.

Marguerite had not heard Thomas move quietly behind her as she spoke on the phone. But when she felt his presence, she spun around and, without provocation, he slapped her hard across the face. She was shocked, bewildered! No one had ever done that to her, not even Thomas. It was so totally unexpected and out of character.

An instant later Marguerite was screaming! Thomas was repeatedly hitting her on the head with the gun.

With each savage, brutal blow, it was as though he was saying,

"Die, Die, Die!"

"Oh God! What is happening to me?" thought Marguerite.

Bleeding profusely and in great pain her only thought now was *escape*. Where?

Screaming, streams of blood running down her face, Marguerite ran towards the half bath hoping to lock the door behind her. Thomas managed to squeeze in with her and in that confined space they struggled. Her screams for help went unanswered. Facing death, Marguerite's will to live gave her extraordinary strength. Thomas had the gun pointed at her chest. With all her energy she twisted his arm, forcing the gun away from herself. A deafening shot rang out shattering the window. Still struggling, but now weakened from the loss of blood and emotional strain, Marguerite was no longer able to hold his arm as tightly. Thomas pulled the trigger again. The bullet pierced her right wrist, traveled the length of her bent arm and exited through the back of her upper arm. Marguerite felt an indescribable, searing, burning pain, like being ripped apart. She heard a click, then .... *silence.*

Marguerite's reactions were automatic, survival instinct, no time to think. Despite the blood blinding her and the excruciating pain, she managed to open the front door and run to the neighbors, each step leaving a trail of blood.

By the time she reached their doorstep, Marguerite was in shock. Her muddled thoughts told her,

"It is unreal!"

"It didn't happen to me, Marguerite!"

"It is only a nightmare."

"I am going to wake up and everything will be OK."

But it was *real!*

The next thing Marguerite remembered clearly, was that she was in an ambulance, sirens blaring, rushing her to a nearby hospital with the young, kind attendant holding her hand and comforting her. In the emergency room the nurses started cutting Marguerite's clothes away, which were soaked with blood.

"You can't do that," protested Marguerite,

"I need my uniform to go to work."

She was definitely *alive!*

Shot, in shock, in pain, she was worried about her uniform! Even tragic moments have their own lighter side. One could not blame the nurses for chuckling. During the examination they discovered that the bullet had also grazed her chest.

The usual questions were asked; next of kin to be notified? Her only family member was her nephew, Danny, who was now living in California. Marguerite gave them the Cramers' telephone number.

As soon as Mark received the telephone call from the hospital, he ran to Hal's coffee shop. Excited and out of breath, he could only say,

"He did it!"

"Who did what?" asked Hal.

"Thomas shot her! He came back, I thought he was in New York".

They rushed to the townhouse and arrived just as the police were taking Thomas away.

That evening Irene and Mark visited Marguerite in the hospital,

"She didn't appear bad. Her arm was completely bandaged, but she was still in shock," recalls Irene,

"Her main concern was for Youki's safety. She asked us to take care of her. In order to get the dog we had get permission from the Scottsdale police to enter the townhouse. No key was available. We wanted to talk to Thomas who was held in one of the cells but they would not let us see him. We were told that his clothes had been taken away because the police were afraid that he would commit suicide. No keys were found with his belongings."

After getting permission from the police, the Cramers went to the townhouse. When they arrived, Irene went first to the garden and tried the arcadia door, it slid open. As she walked in, followed by Mark, she was faced by a growling, snarling poodle. Irene talked softly to the dog, calming her down. She was able to pick Youki up and take her home with them.

Before Marguerite was released from the hospital, the Cramers and Wagners went to clean the townhouse and the sidewalk.

"Walking into the bathroom gave us the impact of the *savage attack.* How much blood she had lost! It was splattered up to the ceiling," recalls Irene. "Seeing the gory sight made Beth feel sick to her stomach."

> "A real friend is one who walks in
> when the rest of the world walks out."
> Walter Winchell

From her hospital bed, Marguerite called Danny. Horrified he could only say,

"How could he stoop so low?!!"

He offered to fly to Arizona, but Marguerite discouraged him. She was concerned that the time off would jeopardize his new job. Visits from the Cramers and Wagners lifted her spirits. They were not just fair weather friends. It was quite a test.

That same day, Thomas was brought up on charges;

ASSAULT WITH INTENT TO COMMIT MURDER
violation of Sec. 13-248, A. R. S. 1956.
Bail set at ten thousand (10,000) dollars.
Enc. Complaint, Warrant, Indigent oath.

Thomas signed a sworn statement,
"I solemnly swear that I am without funds or property with which to employ counsel for my defense in the above captioned case."

The records also show a sworn statement, signed by Thomas that same day, stating that he had been under treatment for a mental condition, and had a history of mental disturbance.

July 22nd

An officer of The Justice Court of Scottsdale Precinct, County of Maricopa, State of Arizona, visited Marguerite at the hospital. She would have to appear in court at 9:00a.m. the following day for the preliminary hearing. An unmarked car would pick her up.

Marguerite cried, pleaded, begged, she didn't want to go. She didn't want to see Thomas again. How could she face that horrible man? The man who had tried to take her life, which was not his to take. She was not given a choice.

But she had no clothes! Marguerite had arrived at the hospital wearing her uniform. It had been discarded, together with her shoes, soaked with blood. She called her girlfriend, Gwen, who picked up some clothes at the townhouse. She had met Gwen at the airport, both were ticket agents working the night shift. Their respective airlines counters were adjacent to each other and when not busy they would chat.

Gwen remembers,

"One time Marguerite invited me to her house. Due to a toothache I was not able to go. I never met her husband because shortly after, they separated. A rare comment Marguerite made about him was that he was very possessive. I was stunned when I saw the television news! When the news spread throughout the airport that she had been shot, we were all shocked. In those days shootings were unheard of. Why did it happen? When I went to see her at the hospital, I offered to stay with her after her discharge. Even though I was scared, and my mother was worried about my safety, I could not let her stay alone. She would need someone to help her dress and mostly to give her moral support. Still, Marguerite gave me the feeling that she was going to go on with her life."

"A faithful friend is the medicine of life."
Eclessiates 6:16

In all the confusion, when Gwen had picked up clothes for Marguerite she had forgotten to bring shoes. Slippers had to be purchased at the hospital gift shop. Sarah, a hospital volunteer, heard about Marguerite's appearance in court. She went to her room,

"Who is going to court with you?" Sarah asked.

"No one," replied Marguerite.

"Then I'll go with you."

Marguerite was overwhelmed by that caring gesture. In her state of turmoil, fear and nervousness, Sarah was an angel of mercy.

Because Marguerite was so nervous, the doctor ordered a strong tranquilizer. During the short drive to the courthouse, Marguerite still could not believe what was happening to her. Her thoughts like a broken record kept repeating again and again,

"I am going to wake up, it is worst than a nightmare. It can't be true!

But, it was all *so true!*

I should not have to go through all this. I hurt, I am tired, I want to be in my hospital bed. I want to jump out of this car and run, run anywhere, get lost and never come back."

Marguerite felt sick in her soul, she desperately wanted to erase this tragedy from her mind.

July 23rd

Realty had to be faced. Very weak and wearing her oversized hospital slippers, her discolored arm in a sling and shuffling along as she leaned on Sarah, Marguerite made a pitiful entrance into the courtroom.

The proceedings started before the Honorable James D. Wilbur, Justice of the Peace. For the State, Robert W. Smithson, Deputy County Attorney and for the Defendant, Benjamin R. Boscoe, Attorney at Law. Julie Adams was duly sworn as the Official Court Reporter.

Thomas came in escorted by a policeman. It took all of Marguerite's willpower not to scream at him,

"How could you? What kind of a beast are you?"

The shock of seeing his face was unbearable.

The preliminary hearing began.

Mr. SMITHSON:

The state will proceed by calling its witness Mrs. Marguerite McGuire.

THE COURT:

It will be necessary for you to take an oath. Will you use your left hand. (Marguerite could not use her wounded right hand). You have been called as a State witness in this case.

Direct examination:

Q - Please state your name.

A - *Marguerite McGuire*

Q - Can you speak up so the Court Reporter can hear you, please?

A - *Marguerite McGuire*

Q - Are you acquainted with the defendant, Thomas McGuire?

A - *Yes*

Q - Is he in the courtroom today?

A - *Yes*

Q - Would you point him out, please?

Marguerite thought, "Oh! why do I have to point, I don't want to look at him!" She raised her left hand to point toward Thomas. The effort of identifying him was emotional torture, it left Marguerite drained.

MR. SMITHSON:

May the record show she indicated the defendant.

The painful examination went on until she was asked,

Q - Can you describe the gun?

A - *No*

Q - Did he point it at you?

A - *I forget, but he asked, "You have to tell me who put you up to this"*

Q - Now, after he showed you the letter that
you testified to, what else did he say
during the struggle, if anything?
A - *I don't remember*
Q -You don't remember?
A - *I was defending myself*

Haltingly, in a trembling voice, Marguerite related all she could remember of those horrifying moments which had happened so quickly.

The court records show that after Marguerite's testimony, Benjamin Waltenberg, police sergeant, City of Scottsdale was called to the stand. He testified that he picked up a small .25 caliber automatic pistol and a clip. Robert Smithson asked him to repeat the conversation he had with the defendant.

SERGEANT WALTENBERG:

"He stated that he arrived in Scottsdale early morning of the 17th.....taken a plane from New York and from Tucson to Phoenix.....rented an apartment in Scottsdale, later had gone to a department store to buy the gun........Later in the day, he went over to her apartment.....waited for her at the back arcadia door. Before getting out of his vehicle he had loaded the weapon with some bullets.....he waited for her to come out of the arcadia door.....when she came out of the arcadia door he pushed her back in."

After further testimony Waltenberg added,

"After two shots he tried again but was unable...it had jammed. I asked him if he intended to kill her, he stated that he did intend. She didn't want him anymore....this was the only thing he could see to do."

CROSS EXAMINATION by Boscoe:

Q - When you were speaking to him describe, what impression he made.

A - *Emotional*

Q - Did he make any threats of any kind while he was talking to you?

A - *Only two, about his wife*

(Waltenberg was not asked what they were)

Following Sergeant Waltenberg's testimony, Police officer Driscoll was called to the stand as a witness for the defendant.

OFFICER DRISCOLL:

"We received a call a little bit after 2p.m. on the 17th, that a man had shot a woman. When I arrived at the given address, the door was ajar, walked in. I found a man who admitted that he had shot his wife. He said that he was not, *nuts.* I looked around for a body or how badly she might be injured. She was found at the neighbors, a towel wrapped around her arm."

Q - "Did you have a conversation with the defendant?"

A - *"He said that he had received a letter from his wife's lawyer stating that he was crazy and he might as well prove it. He later said that; 'Gee, he wished he had went ahead and got the job done!'*

During the cross examination, Officer Driscoll testified that when he had examined the gun he found a jammed shell. Three bullets were still in the clip, an Italian-made gun which holds six to seven rounds.

Q - "Did you find expended casings?" asked Boscoe.

A - *"No, the bathroom was covered with blood. I secured the area and waited for the Detective Sergeant"*

After her testimony, Marguerite was driven back to the hospital, hoping that her eyes would *never* rest on Thomas' face again. She was spared listening to the rest of the court proceedings. Her energy sapped, Marguerite was eagerly content to be back in her hospital bed.

Lana, Marguerite's roommate in the hospital, had been of great help with her personality and sense of humor. On one of her husband's daily visits he brought two bottles of wine and glasses. The following day, Lana and Marguerite secretly polished off one of the bottles. They were thirsty! Some time later, a nurse making her medication rounds saw Lana, mouth opened, snoring loudly.

"What's wrong with her?" she asked.

"I dunno." answered Marguerite with a slurred voice.

How many patients get drunk in a hospital? Despite the circumstances that led Marguerite to that bed, Lana made her laugh. It was contagious. When peas were on the menu, eating them left-handed was a feat. Many landed on the floor. As Marguerite didn't know the extent of the injury to her right hand, she started spending many hours practicing trying to write with her left hand.

August 10th

Marguerite, still recovering at home, received a call from her sister. Her dear papa was terminally ill. It was imperative for her to go to France if she wanted to see him alive. Her supervisor made the necessary arrangements for Marguerite to fly home. It was quite an eventful, emotionally draining trip. On her way from Orly airport to Austerlitz railway station for the eight-hour train ride to her hometown, her cab was stopped by the police. A murderess was on the loose. The "flick" asked for identification, he was suspicious of a woman alone, with a discolored hand and an American passport who spoke French fluently. After explaining the purpose of her journey, Marguerite was waved through. She breathed a sigh of relief.

At home, Marguerite did everything she could to hide her injury from Maman and the family. Despite the summer temperature she wore long sleeves and a sweater over her arm and hand. Maman had enough to bear and didn't need to hear about her personal tragedy. It was difficult smiling, talking with her family like nothing had happened. What mattered most was seeing Papa alive. It gave her peace of mind.

August 16th

Plea of NOT GUILTY

The court ordered that Thomas be examined by two psychiatrists.

September 10th

Thomas was seen by Dr. Sam J. Freenbaum.

Excerpts from his report;

Patient admitted that he snooped around his wife, thinking there was another man. A pattern not uncommon following divorce proceedings. Conclusion was that Thomas McGuire revealed disorders of content but does present a passively dependent relationship with his wife. No evidence of hallucinatory nor delusionary disturbance. Subject quite able to assist counsel in his own defense.

September 28th

Thomas withdrew his non guilty plea to GUILTY to the Amended Information charging Assault With A Deadly Weapon, a Felony

Imposition of sentence, 13th of October 1:30PM

A.R.S 13-249

October 1st

Marguerite's sister called. Papa had died. How much more could happen in such a short period. When Maman was told about the shooting she wrote, "You should have told me about it. I am your mother!" In later years Marguerite and her mother became very close. Even though in early years they had not understood each other, they wrote each other weekly letters for two decades. Her death two years later severed a special tie she still had to the past.

October 4th

Thomas was seen by Dr. George Hastings.

Excerpts from his report;

He had no evidence of any previous mental disorder. At the present time there is no indication of abnormal ideas or psychotic manifestations. He understand his present situation, the charges against him and the difference between right and wrong.

"Work could cure anything,
I believe then, and I believe now."
A Moveable Feast, Ernest Hemingway

During these difficult times, Marguerite again found solace in her work. It helped her to partially put aside her obsessive thoughts. When she had returned to work, the Station Manager called her into his office and offered his support. Marguerite could not believe his kind gesture,

"You can stay with my family for a while."

Her immediate supervisor scolded her,

"Why didn't you tell me that you were having problems with Thomas?"

She had never been able to talk about them, it would have meant admitting defeat. A *happy* facade kept people at bay.

When Marguerite went back to work at the airport ticket counter, she was often on guard, terrified when a look alike Thomas with reddish blond hair was within her range of vision. To make matters worse an agent had transferred from another city, she could not believe it! Walt had the same coloring and build as Thomas. It did not help to chase those awful moments away. The pain in her hand was a constant reminder. Pressure was needed to write the airline tickets so that all carbon copies were legible. It was agony.

When she was slow, Burt would quip,
"She's been winged." His sense of humor eased her emotional pain.

After Gwen left, Marguerite felt very lonely in the townhouse. She was often tense, on the alert and fearful. She knew Thomas was in jail, but the least noise made her jumpy. A car back firing would panic Youki, who would hide under a piece of furniture. Still it was comforting to have her poodle around. Youki gave her unconditional love.

Marguerite knew that she could not possibly live in the townhouse, her sanity was at stake. She was constantly reliving those horrible moments. Passing in front of the closed bathroom door where she had nearly died was unbearable. The townhouse represented a door to the past, one which she wanted to close at any cost. She wanted to bulldoze it, to raze it! The solution was to find a buyer who would assume the mortgage, but she would have to wait until the divorce decree was final, at which time, she would be awarded ownership, but when would that be?

Marguerite decided that it would be worth making double payments, townhouse mortgage and rent. A small price to pay for emotional peace. In late August, Marguerite and Youki moved to the adult apartment complex where Gwen lived. A one bedroom flat was large enough. Now she needed to slowly bring some sort of normalcy into her life.

Marguerite didn't know how to deal with her emotions, she cut the bridges of the past. As grateful as she was for the Cramers and the Wagners' exceptional friendship, seeing them again was too painful. They were constant reminders of her tragedy and a past she so desperately wanted to forget. She stopped calling.

Settled in her new apartment, Marguerite started receiving daily non-threatening letters from Thomas. *Oh-no!* She had thought that the bars of the jail would keep Thomas at bay. She was sadly mistaken. He was haunting her, invading her fragile sense of temporary peace, reminding Marguerite of her *duties* toward him. After all she had been a nurse and should take care of him. Her old 1944 French Red Cross nurse's training. He also suggested that they get back together?!!

After the ATTEMPTED MURDER?!!!

He was not going to hurt her.

Marguerite's doctor suggested that the letters should remain unopened and discarded. Would she ever get any peace, or be able to relax? From that time on she angrily tore the letters into tiny, tiny little pieces. She gathered all the photo albums, giving his photographs the same treatment. She never wanted to see his face, even in print, ever again. All visible traces of him had to go.

Gabrielle, her former neighbor, came to visit. Marguerite thought to inquire about her health. No, she was there to present her with a bill for the cleaning of their blood stained carpeting.

"You have insurance. They will pay for it," she callously told her.

Marguerite was not about to embarrass herself explaining the reasons for the cleaning bill to her insurance agent. To get rid of her, she wrote a personal check. Anything to close another door to the past.

In early October, Marguerite received a call from a Scottsdale Court Probation Officer. He wanted to set up an appointment. During his visit he asked Marguerite what, in her opinion should be done with Thomas. She strongly felt that psychiatric treatment would be more beneficial than a prison term.

Marguerite requested that he be extradited from the state of Arizona and not call, write, or get in touch with her in any sort of a way. If he did, he would have to return to jail. Also, that he be released from jail only after the divorce decree was final. Marguerite told him that she would send a $5.000 check, half of their savings, to David Frank their New York attorney. It would be put into trust to be used for Thomas' psychiatric treatment. Marguerite was trying to think of all ways possible to protect her future.

October 14th, 1965

SENTENCING:

Suspended sentence for five years

Required to return forthwith to the State of New York. Not to leave the state without permission of the Probation Officer of the court.

You will not seek out your former wife, remain away from her, not communicate with her during the term of the probation. Submit immediately to psychiatric treatment until released. Place all your funds and monies in trust with David Frank, Attorney. You will be released in custody of your brother-in-law, who will make monthly reports to the court.

November 2nd

Marguerite's request to the court had been ratified, her divorce decree finalized. Thomas was released from jail. He immediately left Arizona bound for New York.

Marguerite hoped and prayed that the terms of the sentence, the extradition, and the psychiatric treatment for Thomas would keep him out of her life. The divorce didn't ease the pain, Marguerite was changed for life. She looked forward to leading a more peaceful life.

The buyer for the townhouse had also been waiting for that day. Marguerite had taken a drastic step, she sold it for a dollar, with the buyer assuming the mortgage. Another major step in her difficult journey, another door closed. She only wanted peace.

During those trouble times, Marguerite had not been aware that with the divorce proceedings she could have had her name changed. It had been repulsive to have his name on her uniform name tag. She had refused to wear it. Marguerite contacted the courthouse and scheduled an appointment with a judge. After a few questions her request was immediately granted. She reverted to her maiden name, she was now Miss Branquet. A name difficult to pronounce. At the airport the *boys* gently teased her for not choosing, for their convenience a more common name.

"A journey of 1000 miles starts with a single step."
Old proverb

Chapter 6

"A ship in the harbor is safe, but
that is not what ships are built for."
Shedd

After Thomas' release Marguerite's fears increased. She was an *attempted murder survivor.* She had been a front page item, an object of curiosity.

What kind of a future did she have? What was ahead of her? Marguerite felt shut off from other human beings. All alone, without help, she went on.

"She started to make a circle of friends around her," remembers Gwen. What she didn't know was that Marguerite was leading a fake, superficial social life. At the pool she met other singles. She started being invited to parties and even had some of her own.

Within a couple of months, Gwen, her neighbor Sam, Marguerite and another acquaintance, Sandra, formed a foursome. Sundays they would take turns cooking a full meal, elegantly served, along with wine. Their weekly get-together, gave them a resemblance of family life. In spite of those friendships Marguerite felt terribly lonely.

> "Don't be afraid to go out on the limb.
> That's were the fruit is."
>
> unknown

Work and parties were not enough to fill Marguerite's life. As always, the only way she knew how to cope was to keep busy. Her legendary Basque vitality was a plus. In 1966, an opportunity came her way. TWA employees were offered free college tuition, the criteria was to maintain a "B" average. Marguerite's secondary education had been interrupted by circumstances beyond her control, the 1940 German occupation. She could think of many excuses not to take advantage of this opportunity, English was not her mother tongue, her job entailed shift work and she was not familiar with the American educational system. On the other hand, more true to her nature, she thought "Why not?" "Another challenge!" She decided to try.

Marguerite was planning for her future, at one point in her life she might want to change careers. She chose a French major with an English minor, it could lead to teaching opportunities. She had never been on a college campus. It was captivating mingling with those young people, standing in line with them to register, buying used books. It was not an easy task working full-time and taking nine credit hours. She would go to the library and come out with her arms full of books for term paper research. Writing them created a problem, she had never written one before. The floor around her typewriter would be littered with crumpled sheets of paper.

Everything was a first. At the end of the third semester, Marguerite received a letter from Arizona State University President's office, advising her that she had made the Dean's List. Wow! Marguerite had reached for the fruit! She had left the harbor.

With her schedule of work, school, travel and keeping up her single household. Marguerite didn't have much time to think. She wanted to forget and anesthetize herself.

As 1966 was coming to and end, Marguerite had hesitantly accepted a blind date for a New Year's party. Willard would pick her up after her three to midnight shift. The new year, 1967, only 15 minutes old, brought him to the door. The doorbell made her jump. It was scary, what would that man look like? Slowly she opened the door. Youki greeted him like a long lost friend, it was a good omen. Marguerite found herself facing a tall, dark-haired, extremely masculine looking man with an engaging smile. From that moment on a special magnetism attracted them to each other. It didn't take long for a serious relationship to develop.

At the apartment complex parties they were considered a couple. It had been hard for Marguerite to let him penetrate the wall she had built around herself and enter her world of pain and distrust. She didn't want to be hurt again. Fear of rejection had driven her deeply into her world of emotional isolation. After the shooting her view of the world had been distorted. How could she trust again?

With her sense of *fair play,* Marguerite revealed the 1965 tragedy. Dating her could put Willard's life in danger. Thomas had said,

"If I can't have you, nobody else will!"

He was free in New York, no barriers except a court order. No guarantee that he would not violate the terms of his probation and return to Phoenix. A very dangerous cloud hanging over them like Damocles' sword. Willard had choice words for people like Thomas, "I won't let the b.....d touch you!" he was already showing his protective nature. It didn't faze him a bit.

Both divorced, they were very cautious of emotional involvement. Besides Willard being 5'9" and handsome, Marguerite had been attracted by his caring personality. Their love slowly blossomed. A year and half later, in May of 1968, they were married.

Trust is a solid foundation.

Marguerite felt safe with Willard, her fears receded. They started leading a busy life of work, real estate ventures, and enjoying his children's bi-monthly visits. Summer vacations taken with them were fun. They flew to many exotic places; the Virgin Islands, La Paz and many European countries were visited. Jerry and Jane became a balm in Marguerite's childless life.

Due to her 6:00 a.m. shift at the airport, Marguerite's bedtime hours didn't follow the norm. Retiring early was a necessity. One spring evening in 1969, she kissed Willard good-night, and went to bed leaving him watching the evening news. An hour later he heard an unusual groan coming from the bedroom. He rushed to investigate. *SHOCK!* Totally taken by surprise, he found Marguerite in the throes of a grand mal seizure.

When Marguerite came to she could not understand why she was partially clothed. Before going to bed she had put her nightclothes on. Willard had been trying to dress her to take her to the hospital.

"What's going on?" asked a bewildered Marguerite.

"You had a seizure" a concerned Willard answered.

"I had *what*? *A seizure*?"

"It can't, it can't possibly be true!" she repeatedly told herself. She was so ashamed that Willard had seen her in that condition. What would he think? They had barely been married one year. Control was very important to Marguerite, losing it was a disaster.

On the way to the hospital her mind was in turmoil, she had no previous history of seizures. "What's happening to me?" she asked herself. After all she was in excellent health. Her hospital was stay was of short duration. The Doctor was not overly concerned. He stated that the EEG was not abnormal for a woman her age. It was thought to be a one time occurrence.

Willard and Marguerite resumed their busy life putting the incident in the back of their mind. A year later she had another nocturnal seizure.

"No, No, No! Not again," thought Marguerite.

A very concerned Willard took her to the hospital. A neurologist was called, diagnosis - epilepsy! Thomas' murderous attack. The horrendous, multiple, savage blows to her head had brought on the seizures, he was going to haunt her forever. Could she ever forget him? Would she ever have peace of mind? Marguerite was angry, she wanted to curse him. From that day on Marguerite and Willard's lives were effected for ever, but they had each other.

"I am not permitted to hate."

Terry Anderson (former hostage in Lebanon)

The doctor prescribed medication and recommended she refrain from drinking alcohol or caffeine and taking stimulants or anti-depressants. Following his advice Marguerite would be able to lead a seizure-free life. Now, she had to take medication for the rest of her life. She didn't want to face an incurable disorder caused by Thomas. Another stumbling block in Marguerite's emotional healing.

Marguerite soon realized that epilepsy, with all its myths, was a very lonely disorder. Another kind of fear invaded her life. Night after night,

"Will it happen again?" she asked herself.

Dr. Edward Faught, M. D., and the Director of the University of Alabama Epilepsy Center states,

"Society's misunderstanding of epilepsy extracts a toll on the individual. A disorder very much misunderstood, often causing more emotional problems than physical. We've learned that seizure control by itself does not necessarily translate into an improved quality of life."

The medication prescribed had many side effects, one of them, disruptive mood swings. That would not do. Her neurologist prescribed a more suitable anti-convulsant.

What about her job? She was afraid she would lose it.

How would she tell her supervisor?

When Marguerite had the courage to tell him, he stammered,

"Epi-lep-sy?"

His next comment was even more comforting,

"My dog has seizures!"

"What will I do if you have a seizure behind the ticket counter?"

Very calmly Marguerite answered,

"Well, I'll fall. But don't worry, the floor is carpeted. You can take care of my line of passengers!"

His worst fears never materialized. Thirteen years later, by retirement date, having completed thirty years of service, Marguerite had not had another seizure.

One day at work, one of her co-workers playfully tapped her on the shoulder from behind. Marguerite turned around to strike him. Her reaction had been automatic, controlled by the fear still lingering deep within her. She was still trying to defend herself from an attack. That was the start of many similar occurrences.

In 1970, Willard and Marguerite went to Spain to visit her niece who had married a Spaniard. During their stay they visited Madrid's famous market place. As they walked leisurely, looking at the stalls with their various merchandise, a man rudely bumped her. Marguerite became irrationally angry. Willard became upset with her as he didn't understand. Marguerite didn't fully understand it herself. It had been another unconscious reaction to Thomas' blows.

Shortly after her second seizure, an intruder, not a stranger, started invading Marguerite's nights. *Thomas.* He appeared in her dreams, stalking her from doorways, lurking through windows. She would wake up screaming! But Willard was always there to calm her, take her in his arms and comfort her,

"I am here, you have nothing to fear."

He was a pillar of strength. Even the nights didn't set her free. Those nightmares would leave her emotionally drained and would reinforce her fears.

If Marguerite heard an unusual noise during the night, she would wake up with a start and sit up, tense, every fiber of her body taut! Mind on *alert.*

"Willard, I heard a noise!"

Sleepily he would answer,

"I am sure it is nothing, go back to sleep."

But Marguerite would beg him,

"Please, please check the doors!"

Patiently he would get up. Always a false alarm. Her fears might have seemed irrational, but they were very real. It could not have been easy for Willard to deal with her mood swings and her fears. He was a forgotten caregiver.

Acceptance didn't come easily, but Marguerite was not a person to wallow in self-pity. Still, people have the right to ask themselves,

"Why me?"

In Sweet Reprieve, Frank Maier states,

"People who stoically shoulder their pain without asking, Why me?, are missing the chance to enrich their own lives and the lives of those around them. They are failing to look for the promise that lies hidden just beneath the surface of every heartbreak."

Life went on.

After her marriage to Willard, Marguerite had stopped her college education. In 1975, her stepson Jerry, after seeing one of Marguerite's drawings, urged her to return to college. He was handing her a *key*. A good key! Art had always been appealing. She enrolled in a commercial art class. Soon her talents came forth, pen & ink drawings turned into designed note paper. Now she was happily juggling homemaking, a full time job and college. Later she was attracted by another brilliant *key,* an ad in her church bulletin, OIL PAINTING CLASSES. One evening a week would not be too much. What a revelation! From her brush strokes on the canvas came myriads of colors, birds, flowers and landscapes. Painting became a channel to express some of her feelings and get lost in her new found release. A place Thomas *never* invaded.

Good years passed. Marguerite had a caring husband, loving step-children, whom she watched grow and eventually leave for their respective careers. During all those years Marguerite had religiously taken her medication, refrained from taking anything that could possibly bring on another seizure. It was a good life.

In 1981 Willard and Marguerite started thinking about their retirement years. They had been around the world and visited many European countries. Now their plans were to see the United States in a camper trailer, traveling at their own pace.

May 1982

Retirement!

Marguerite happily put her uniform to pasture. Willard closed his business and now would have more time to devote to their real estate ventures. They spent many evenings sitting on their living room floor, maps of the United States spread in front of them. They could see themselves leisurely driving through back roads, eating in small town diners. A major stop would be visiting Willard's birth place in Kansas.

In the fall of 1983 Willard started complaining about a lump in his side. Spring 1984, Marguerite had to rush Willard to the hospital. His left kidney was removed encased in a cancerous tumor. What a shock! During their 15 years of marriage Willard had never been sick.

The Doctor was optimistic, Willard was going to be OK. Their retirement life resumed, the word cancer relegated to the back of their minds. In the fall, their bubble of euphoria broke, cancer cells had spread, a second operation was needed. With a heavy heart Marguerite saw the slow progression of the illness.

March 1985

The oncologist gave them the sad news, a life expectancy of two to six months. By then, the spark in Willard's eyes was a thing of the past. It broke Marguerite's heart. Their old age plans would never materialize, their dreams destroyed by cancer.

Marguerite had the thankless job of caring for Willard. Few remember the caregiver, who often is the person shouldering the most stress and fatigue. Caregiving, added responsibilities, were taking their toll on Marguerite. The strain at times, was overwhelming.

She went to see her new physician who was not familiar with epilepsy, he prescribed tranquilizers. In her state of mind, and physically, emotionally and psychologically depleted, Marguerite took the pills. The result, her third nocturnal grand mal seizure. She was devastated. She needed to be well to care for Willard. The tranquilizers were discarded.

After a long battle with cancer, peacefully, Willard died September 12, 1985. Marguerite had given him loving care to the end of his life. Now she was alone. She felt utterly weary and grief-stricken.

"It dawned on me that the most important thing he'd said was his farewell. He was actually going into the real world."

Acts of Faith, Erich Segal

Willard had touched her life so deeply. She had her memories, she could not be the *new* Marguerite had she not known him. With his philosophy of life which he so freely shared, Willard left her a legacy. He had been the center of her world and she had lost it. She had choices, she chose to live. Very slowly and painfully life went on.

"Life is life, fun is fun,
but all is quiet when the goldfish dies."
Ancient Coptic

Chapter 7

"Often the test for courage is not to die, but to live."
Alfieri

Willard's death had been like an engulfing tornado, a quake followed by many small ones. Marguerite's husband, her protector, friend and family was gone. During the last months of his life Willard's often repeated words came to her mind,

"What is going to happen to you?"

Why would he say that? It seemed strange. He knew that she was self-sufficient, capable of taking care of herself. True to his protective nature, to the end of his life he showed concern for Marguerite's safety. It was his last parting gift.

During their marriage, Willard had given her a sense of security. The shooting, or the possibility of Thomas' return, had not been mentioned again. They loved each other, had a new life to lead. Marguerite's past, they thought, was a closed chapter. They never knew if he was alive or not. His presence though, was felt first with Marguerite's seizures and the intrusions into her nightmares. Silently Willard had worried.

After Willard's death Marguerite threw herself headlong into a frenzy of activities, traveling and involving herself in community service. Thinking was too painful and scary. Willard's death, followed by many other significant losses, reopened the deeply buried, violently inflicted wounds. Fear and hyper-vigilance increased. Her dear nephew Danny died two years after Willard, it was like losing a son. She now felt totally alone.

Our lives are like archways. Each archway is unique. As the years pass stones are lost, damaged or pulverized. At times, in the empty spaces some uneven stones are placed, others repaired with haste. The strong winds of life, storms, hurricanes, tremors shake the archway. They represent life's problems, sicknesses, deaths and tragedies. With each tremor, weak stones fall and cracks widen, weakening the structure. For many reasons some repairs are not done or are rushed by circumstances and the mortar does not hold. The archway's facade looks fine, the empty spots not visible.

Like World War II buildings, some of Marguerite's stones were marked by bullets holes. For nineteen years Willard had been a strong mason on the scaffold with her, his caring solidifying the archway. During those years Marguerite and Willard had their own small quakes, but together, their archway withstood the winds and storms of marriage and life.

Willard had been a cornerstone. His death severely damaged the archway, touching all the stones. Lesser stones fell, piling on top of the bullet damaged stones in a heap. The archway was left without design.

"Memory is a drug. Memory can hold you against your strength and your will."

West of the Night, Beryl Markham

Survivors of traumas need immediate, special, attention. Marguerite survived the best she could and without help. Behind her mask of "insouciance", carefree attitude, Marguerite didn't know how to deal with those resurfacing feelings of fear and hypervigilance. A victim who had not received any help, none had been offered. To this day there are no support groups for attempted murder survivors. They are *forgotten survivors*, reminders of our violent society. It is easier to ignore their needs.

Marguerite had a brush with death. A gun barrel, pointed at her by Thomas, firing bullets. She didn't die. Slowly she realized that her emotional needs could no longer be ignored. Eagerly she searched a way for recovery, to *heal.* Finding the right mason was lengthy, eventually she found a counselor, *hope,* Gary.

"Let the person talk and tell the story," said Freud.

Marguerite told Gary the painful story, exposed her scattered stones. Slowly, he provided ways to find tools, helped her find the proper way to mix the mortar to deal with suppressed feelings. She needed to face the past, the deep rooted damaged parts of the archway behind the veneer. It had been badly abused.

The origin of the bullet holes needed to be acknowledged. Before repairs could be started these stones needed to be examined, the extent of damage assessed, inventory made. Patching needed to be done carefully otherwise those stones might crumble again under the weight of new traumas.

During that period Marguerite's long time friend, Laura died, they had been so close. Even Laura had not been aware of Marguerite's setbacks and the prolonged struggles. Again, a significant heavy stone fell scattering other stones. The empty spots, where baby stones had been cast away as not important, had been pushed away by Thomas, and replacement stones refused. Empty, irreplaceable holes. Only Marguerite could tell how important those losses were.

Gary handed Marguerite a rusty *key,*

"Did you ever see the newspaper article about the shooting?" he asked.

She had not.

He suggested that she go to the Scottsdale Library microfilm section and read the July 19, 1965 Scottsdale Progress issue.

The thought of using the key was scary. It would start the destruction of *amnesia.*

What would she find behind that heavy door? With mixed feelings, Marguerite accepted the key which led her to the library. It was hard pushing the heavy door of the past with its rusty hinges. It had been closed for twenty-seven years.

Would it upset her to read the article?

How would she react?

She found the newspaper and read the front page article which she had never seen. How hard to believe that it was herself. The repressed anger resurfaced, how could Thomas have done such a dreadful act? Plagued her for life?

Several months later Marguerite realized that to continue with her *healing,* she needed to read the trial records. It would pry that door wide open. It took all her emotional strength to go to the County Court House where she obtained the case records. Painfully Marguerite read, she could not believe that Thomas had been remorseless.

He had told the arresting detective that,

" *He wished that he had finished the job!* "

How crass! How revolting!

A cold-blooded, planned murder.

As Marguerite read on she was appalled by one of the documents signed by Thomas. It stated that he was *indigent*! How could he perjure himself? Arizona is a community property state, the townhouse was owned jointly, furthermore, he had his lifetime pension. Marguerite was furious at his unending lack of basic principles. As she read on her anger increased. During his examination, Thomas told one of the psychiatrists that he had wanted Marguerite to,

"Pay for all the trouble she caused him and his parents."

Pay for what?!!

Thomas had agreed to the separation. He had not thought that Marguerite was going to follow through and have him served with divorced papers! He was losing a comfortable life style. For Thomas it was a catastrophe! He had the audacity to bring his parents into the picture. The word parents should have been replaced by *Mother*!

The next official document was a signed statement that Thomas had a mental condition and a history of mental disturbance. By that time, Marguerite was seething. That conniving man! A plea of insanity was pure fabrication. Thomas never had a history of mental illness, and had never been under treatment. He was a very clever man who would go to any length to obtain what he wanted. He was the attacker, the murderer! A suspended sentence, and five years probation, should have been a lifetime. His defense and the psychiatrists were paid for by the taxpayers, and his pension was left untouched.

The victim, Marguerite, was left with an incurable disorder, epilepsy, and the pain in her right hand. She suffered the violation of her body, loss of control and emotional freedom. She now lives her life with a shattered sense of peace. Never to feel completely safe again. Marguerite is excused from jury duty for the rest of her life and isn't able to deal with the violence in many movies or television. *Is that justice?*

With all its horror it had been beneficial for Marguerite to read those records. Release her pent up anger. With Gary's guidance Marguerite started to realize that she was the master mason, repairs were started. At times he would be on the scaffold with her. She is rebuilding, slowly freeing herself of the shackles of the painful past. She is repairing her archway with her own new designs; refashioning it with a mixture of old stones, patched ones and some new ones. It's the start of *healing!*

> "It is not easy to take problems one at the time
> when they refuse to stay in line."
>
> Ashleigh Briliant

Chapter 8

"For only the hand of life
can contain your hearts."
The Prophet, Kahlil Gabran

Attempted murder survivors. Who are they? Could it be the woman on the book cover? A young man on a football field? A derelict? The person in a church pew sitting next to you? An elderly person? Anyone of them could. They can come from all walks of life, from the richest to the poorest. Their emotional scars do not show. Can they live at peace or is their trauma dragging them like a ball and chain? They are like wounded soldiers returning from different wars. Their wounds and scars less visible than those who lost a leg or an arm. But, the battle scars are still there. Victims are often blamed and judged without court or trial.

What did Marguerite do to provoke him?

They must have had a quarrel!

She must have had a lover!

Without provocation.

With premeditation

Thomas came to the townhouse to kill her.

It happened so fast! No time to quarrel. No lover for Marguerite, it would have been against her moral principles.

Dr. Sam J. Freenbaum had stated in his report that Thomas thought that there was a man involved. A very common accusation in a divorce case.

On July 17, 1965, Thomas flew from New York to Scottsdale, Arizona to take Marguerite's most precious possession, *her life!*

He pulled a trigger several times, Marguerite fiercely fought, she survived. Her destiny was not in his hands. In Thomas' eyes her life had no value, it could be discarded at will with a weapon.

He believed that Marguerite was his, a possession,

"She is mine!"

Thomas had wanted to destroy her rather than allow another person to have her. On the day of the attack he had told Marguerite,

"If I can't have you nobody else will!"

How could anyone claim her life, it was totally *hers*. No one could own her or could ever possess her. Marguerite was her own person, an individual, different, *unique*. In that difference there is freedom.

"When I say I, I mean absolutely 'unique'
not to be confused with any other."

Hugo Betti

It had been a very well planned premeditated murder attempt by a non-violent man. Why had he flown from New York to Phoenix via Tucson? Because he was avoiding Terminal Number 2 where Marguerite worked. There was also the possibility of being recognized by one of her co-workers. He had rented a car, bought the gun. All well planned, the scenario was complete, left was the execution. She was dazed by Thomas' scheme, the enormity of the crime. The bullet, an intruder, violated her body causing agonizing pain. It left permanent physical scars. She was maimed emotionally and psychologically, very well hidden behind a facade of false peace. No value? Marguerite's life is priceless!

Victims' sentence - Does it ever end?

Repercussions can last a life time. Fear is the most prevalent, a crippler, it can ruin lives. It's no ordinary fear because it was caused by a non-ordinary trauma. Hypervigilance, is similar to the flights of sparrows who scatter at the least movement. These reactions might seem unreasonable to others but are very real for the victim. Repressed anger at the person who committed that vile act, the feeling of helplessness. Shattered sense of peace, security, *never* to feel completely safe again. Marguerite had an overwhelming loss of trust. She was marked for life. Losses so great, that only other attempted murder survivors can understand.

Marguerite had wanted to build a wall where Thomas could not find her. He pursued her in her sleep, left indelible traces. Willard had often been her shield.

Despite her good friends' help, the Cramers, the Wagners and Gwen who had been there for her she had felt isolated, tainted. The crime had cut her off from the rest of the world.

Victims have different residue intensity based on the impact of the trauma and past significant losses. Still they have common threads. Their grief is not addressed and is not always associated with death. What you don't grieve gets buried alive. The bereaved need compassion, survivors need lifetime compassion.

It was in the middle 1980's that PTSD, Post Traumatic Stress Disorder was formally acknowledged.

Excerpts from the 1991, winter issue of ICAL, of Dr. Alice L. Cullinan, Ph.D, a journal on trauma, confirms Marguerite's reactions and emotions; loss of self-esteem, intrusive nightmares, recurrent dreams and flight into activity. These conditions can last a lifetime.

Platitudes, cliches, add to the sense of helplessness. Over the years Marguerite has often been told,

"Why should you feel so bad, after all, you could have been killed, left crippled!"

To this day she still hears other inane platitudes,

"You are so lucky you are still alive,"

"You function well."

Marguerite could not associate the shooting with luck. The damage is unseen!

"Think of all the people who are worse off than you are." These cliches amounted to,

"You don't deserve to feel bad."

"The strongest words are thoughts we do *not*, the most important comment can often be silence and the greatest sign of caring is simply listening."

Roger Downey, KPHO-TV, Phoenix, Az

(from the preface of Platitudes, You are not me! by Maita Floyd)

Why are people's traumas minimized? There are no yardsticks, scales, or classification of who deserves to be listened to or ignored. People can measure their own pain but not *others.*

"Some phlegmatic people are able to bear a very
heavy burden without breaking under the strain;
for others, the load of tension must be lighter
if the mind is to sustain its balance."

Peace of Mind, Joshua Loth Liebman

Marguerite's past losses had added to the impact of her emotional trauma;

Absentee parents, lack of nurturing

Separation - boarding schools

Loss of home during the German occupation

Interrupted education

Miscarriages

Divorce

Willard's death

Danny and her best friend Laura's death

So much unresolved grief, too many consecutive significant deaths, delayed reactions. Marguerite needed comfort of mind, body and soul. Her greatest help had been her spirit of survival.

In 1965 Marguerite had a new lease on life, more people to love, many more things to see and accomplish. She had, "A world without walls."

Chapter 9

"I often have been adrift, but I always stayed afloat."
The Whales of August, David Berry

Several months after Willard's death Marguerite met a caring woman, Edith. She was compassionate, patiently listened, and encouraged her.

"You have a lot to tell and offer," said Edith, "write a book about your life's experiences, help others."

"You can't be serious!" retorted Marguerite

Their exceptional friendship was of short duration, loss again - Edith died. But, she had tossed her a *key* to a door she didn't know existed. A *key* to a magical door, opening to a room which would lead to many other rooms.

Marguerite had dared many times before, she could again. Willard's often repeated words would ring in her mind, *You have guts!*

She also had perseverance and boldness. Edith had helped her strengthen her archway, propped it up with her friendship when it was ready to collapse.

"He had left me a word, a key to a door I never knew was there, and still had to find."

West of the Night, Beryl Markham

Edith's words had grown into a thought, to an idea, to an act. My short friendship with Edith had a tremendous impact on my life says, author Maita Floyd. After her death her kind voice would ring in my ears, "write, write". I finally accepted the *key* she had tossed. Cautiously I opened the door unaware that it would lead to many others. Each new door revealing an unending world of wonders. Like a child I wanted to open all of them at once. Each door etched with new words writing, illustrating and publishing.

It became necessary for me to use the rusty key offered by my counselor Gary. With his help open the painful door of the past, to push it open, look inside and acknowledge its contents. My old wounds were buried alive in the deepest of my being, they needed air to heal. For decades they had been covered by amnesia, never allowing myself to be angry. To me anger was loss of control, I had enough of it in my life. Amnesia had been more convenient. I needed to give voice to the hurt and hate. Had I been acting like Don Quixote fighting my ghosts with a wooden sword? Gary's suggestions were instrumental in the realization that my healing would be to relate my trauma.

I have grown and changed because of all my past experiences, people that I have met, loved during my life. I have been enriched by my willingness to share. I respect and honor my story. My hope is that among my readers, one person in a similar situation, will be helped by my storytelling. You are not alone, we have common bonds. I hope that the other readers will be more understanding and compassionate toward other attempted murder survivors.

"Share your burdens with your friends."
Hebrews 10:24,25

I started to see my journey back to its beginning that has brought me to this point. The culmination of my wounds have helped me to write this book. I have shared my painful experiences and how I rose above my adversities to become a successful writer, artist, lecturer and publisher. A great part of my recovery lays between the covers of this book, my third. The cover is a younger oil self-portrait. My goal is to attain its serene look and inner peace.

Willard had been the most important person in my life, my first *bonding relationship* since Mademoiselle Durcudoy. Willard had a steadfast nature, standing by people whether they were around to know it or not. I lost a channel to my own soul, and the awareness was most devastating. A world of comforting presence, safety, protection and support. My grieving process, complicated by his many roles including as a caregiver. Willard had an unforgettable and transcending influence on my life. He gave me strength, a smile, a touch. He was there for me to lean on.

We all have choices, after Willard's death I chose to go on, pick up the pieces, rebuild my archway. I realized that, like Father Jenco, I need to *heal* the memories.

Life is precious, a continuous challenge, with many *keys* tossed in our direction .

A life is to be live *one day at a time.*

Had I died
I would have not met Willard
who
loved me the way I was
loved him the way he was
we had
spaces in our togetherness
till death parted us

.... *Also by MAITA FLOYD*

Caretakers, the Forgotten People

"A love story in diary fashion written with honesty, understanding, compassion, and courage. A story of hope and survival, and of transcending love"

Jane Murdock, SPEX, Fort Bragg, CA

"A moving story.....her front-cover painting....a bluebird sitting on a branch of life, watching her soaring hopes...her dashed dreams...poignant and devastatingly honest."

Bookreader, Capitola, CA

Platitudes, You are not me!

"If we could hear what we are saying, we would know how words can hurt."

Roger Downey, KPHO-TV, Phoenix, AZ

"A GEM, rather unique...entertaining, but always provocative."

John McComish,
Little Professor Bookstore, Phoenix, AZ

Order Form

Name ______________________________

Address ____________________________

City ____________________ St. ________

Zip _____________

Make check or money order payable to:
Eskualdun Publishers, Ltd.
P.O. Box 50266
Phoenix, Az 85076-0266

To order by phone or for more information call:
1-800-848-1192 or (602) 893-2394

Don't Shoot!
My life is valuable $10.95

Platitudes,
You are not me! $9.95

Caretakers,
the Forgotten People $9.95

Shipping;
one book $2.00
each additional book $1.00

Total Enclosed ......$ ________
(Including Shipping)